Where Is My Caterpillar?

**Written by
Diana Noonan**

**Illustrated by
Isabel Lowe**

Mr. Scott said, "Next week is Bug Week. On Monday, I want you to bring a bug to school to show the class."

That night I looked in
our garden for a bug.
I found a fat green caterpillar
on a cabbage.
I put it in a jar
beside my bed.

But on Monday, it wasn't there!
"It's gone!" I shouted.
"My caterpillar's gone!"

"Has anyone seen my caterpillar?"

"I saw it," said Amy.
"It was crawling along the bathtub. Yuck!"

I ran to the bathtub, but it wasn't there.
"It won't be there now," said Amy.
"I saw it on Friday night."

"Are you looking for your caterpillar?" asked Dad. "It was crawling along the TV set."

I ran to the TV set, but it wasn't there.
"It won't be there now," said Dad.
"I saw it on Saturday morning."

"Are you looking for your caterpillar?" asked Stephen. "I saw it crawling up the kitchen window."

I ran to the kitchen window,
but it wasn't there.
"It won't be there now,"
said Stephen.
"I saw it on Sunday morning."

11

I didn't know what to do.
I didn't have a bug to take to school.

Then Mom asked,
"Are you looking for
your caterpillar?
I saw it crawling up
the washing machine.
It was there this morning."

I ran to the washing machine,
and there it was.
I put my fat green caterpillar
in a jar and took it to school.

14

There were bugs everywhere.
"You've brought a caterpillar,
Sean," said Mr. Scott.
"Where do we find
caterpillars?" he asked the class.
"On cabbages,"
everyone shouted.

"Not this one, Mr. Scott," I smiled.
"I found this one on our washing machine!"